xenophobicracy

ALSO BY NGOZI OLIVIA OSUOHA

The Transformation Train
Letter to My Unborn
Sensation
Tropical Escape (with Amos O. Ojwang')
Fruits from the Poetry Planet
Poetic Grenade
Whispers of the Biafran Skeleton
Chains
Raindrops
Freeborn
Eclipse of Tides
The Subterfuge
Green Snake on a Green Grass
Chariots of Archangels
Wonderment
Interwoven

xenophobicracy

poems by
Ngozi Olivia Osuoha

Poetic Justice Books
Port St. Lucie, Florida

©2020 Ngozi Olivia Osuoha

book design and layout: SpiNDec, Port Saint Lucie, FL
cover design: Kris Haggblom

All rights reserved.

No part of this book may be used or reproduced in any manner whatsoever without written permission except in the case of brief quotations embodied in critical articles and reviews. Members of educational institutions and organizations wishing to photocopy any of the work for classroom use, or authors, artists and publishers who would like to obtain permission for any material in the work, should contact the publisher.

Published by Poetic Justice Books
Port Saint Lucie, Florida
www.poeticjusticebooks.com

ISBN: 978-1-950433-39-1

FIRST EDITION
10 9 8 7 6 5 4 3 2 1

This book is dedicated to the victims of xenophobia, especially all Nigerians killed in South Africa.

contents

- Ubuntu 3
- Songs 4
- Colonialism 5
- Hate 6
- Minerals 7
- Intimidation 8
- Manipulation 9
- Vandalism 10
- Slavery 11
- Greed 12
- Mental Slavery 13
- Crime 14
- Hunger 15
- Riches 16
- They 17
- Strategy 18
- Commotion 19
- Religion 20
- Misplaced Aggression 21
- Experiments 22
- Crime 23
- Sex 24
- HIV AIDS 25
- Rape 26
- Laziness 27
- Assassination 28
- Gangsterism 29
- Marriage 30
- Miners 31
- Racism 32

Promiscuity 33
Single Parenting 34
Prostitution 35
Migration 36
Education 37
Ignorance 38
Immorality 39
Menace 40
Envy 41
Greener Pasture 42
Sacrifice 43
Foreign Control 44
Observers 45
Covetousness 46
Cavemen 47
Rehabilitation 48
Poverty 49
Government 50
False Promises 51
Carelessness 52
Looseness 53
Mandela 54
Apartheid 55
Contributions 56
Young 57

Legitimate 58
Jealousy 59
Robbery 60
Drug Abuse 61
Users and Abusers 62
Owners 63
Diplomacy 64
Suddenly 65
Attacks 66
Burning 67
Looting 68
Women 69
Setting Humans Ablaze 70
Butchering Strangers 71
Stoning 72
Lawless 73
Injustice 74
Police 75
Corpses 76
Unwelcome 77
Bad Governance 78
Shameless Lies 79
Hostage 80
Black on Black Hate 81
Organized Crime 82

Agony 83
Shame 84
Reprisal Attacks 85
Killings 86
Xenophobia 88
Meanwhile 89
Nigeria 90
Borders 91
Qualifications 92
I Am Because You Are 93
Few People 94
Dead Ones 95
Stranded 96
Go Home! Go Home! 97
Allen Onyema 98
Air Peace 99
Victims 100
Returnees 102
Africa 104
Xenophobicracy 105

xenophobicracy

UBUNTU

Ubuntu, Ubuntu
They call you Ubuntu,
They invoke powers
To buttress your spirit,
They chant and dance
They raise a glorious voice
And celebrate your soul
But they are far, far away.

Ubuntu, Ubuntu
They call you unity
They call you peace
They call you love
They call you brotherhood
They call you hospitality
But, they mean hostility.

Ubuntu, Ubuntu
I am because you are
You are because I am
But we are strangers
Aliens of bitterness
Monsters of hate.

SONGS

You sing like angels
And shake mountains
You sing like diverse choirs
Yet minister enmity.

Your voice uproots skyscrapers
You lift burdens
Your prayers travel far
Yet you kill more.

Your songs are hymns
They are psalms
They raise the dead
And enliven the lost
Yet, they pass not your lips.

Songs of partial interests
Deceiving poor souls
Torturing floating spirits
Crucifying meek minds
Haunting mild hearts
O songs of crucifixion.

COLONIALISM

Not only you were colonized
Almost all Africa was,
Others fought for independence
And time liberated them.

They put away some hate
The intents of the master
They made away with bitterness
The rage of the scorpion,
They waved aside the beast
And managed to move on
No matter how they fail.

Poor, poorest of the poor
Though rich, rich and wealthy
Blessed beyond comprehension
Endowed and ordained
Chosen and consecrated
Yet, balanced and archived.

Colonialism taunted Africa
Yes, it did, and still do
But then nothing is constant except change.

HATE

They planted hate
They instilled hatred
They buried envy intermediately
They sowed disunity
They struck the Shepherd
And the flock scattered
So they operated deeply.

They took advantage of all
They harnessed the land
And exploited the vine,
They humiliated the gods
And violated nature,
So they operated deeply.

The hate was within
It was among siblings
It was within kinsmen
Clans and societies
Homes and families
Everything turned upside down
But then, nothing is permanent except change.

MINERALS

They extract minerals
And mine our soul
They explore oil
And gain crude
No challenge, no opposition.

Various gifts, natural
From human to material
Known, unknown, visible, invisible
They pruned, extracted, harvested
Yes, they did.

Set asunder, planted collision
Instilled fear, dug mines
Miners against selves
They worked, truly, they did.

Minerals, upon minerals
Funerals upon funerals
Deaths, fight, wars
Troubles, and dichotomy
Bigotry, vengeance and hate.

INTIMIDATION

Forces, strange and alien
Powers, foreign and raw
Voices; hard and strong
Orders; harsh and common.

Intimidations and frustrations
Intimidating aborigines
Frustrating locals
Organizing crimes
Syndicates and chains
Cells of uninterrupted activities.

Intimidations, raw and hot
Dishing pain and rain
Sharing agony and fight
Trapping a people
Trashing a land
Crushing a nation
Diverse intimidations.

Yes, they manipulated
They manoeuvred
They squandered.

MANIPULATION

Crude manipulations
Highly sophisticated rings
Webs of hard confusion
Complex chess
Complete game
Not leaving anything to chance
Fate, ill-fated, chained.

Ranks of apex torture
Climax devouring
Peak manipulation
Calculated attempts
Concentrated plots
Tactical practices
Practical tactics,
Theories and theorems
Anguish and languishing vandalism
Torturing a land so blessed.

Manipulations, manipulators advancing
Gathering the populace
Entrapping minds and hearts
Engrossing souls in loss.

VANDALISM

Strangers on rampage
Inheriting the land
Dividing the owners
Confusing heirs
Luring and enticing indigenes.

Vandals on raid
Campaigning for war
Destroying future
Shattering peace
Butchering hope,
And burying love.

Vandals in religion
Vandals in politics
Vandals in education
Vandals of civilization.

Vandalization, capped
Vandals, honoured
Vandalization, enthroned
Vandalized people
Vandalized land.

SLAVERY

Africa was real, very real
True and lovely
Lively and contented
Frank and honest
Until slavery came.

Slavery came with hate
Slavery brought greed
It sowed disunity
It imbued bigotry
And scattered lies.

Slavery planted selfishness
It mounted dishonesty,
Slavery built insincerity
It sold betrayal.

Slavery gave low self esteem
It painted black evil,
It severed bonds and friendship
Slavery perpetrated horrors
Indescribable atrocities
Slavery disvirgined Africa.

GREED

Sowed greed, watered enmity
Pruned the farm of lust
Interwoven anger and fight
Bitterness grew, so much.

Bitter soul, angry heart
Vengeful mind, lost hope
Greed, ripped happiness.

The quest to conquer
The zeal to vanquish
The passion to disorganize
The love to destroy
Greed, patrolled all.

Intriguing patterns
Hateful avenues
Ridiculous tricks
Dubious tracks
Personal interests, nothing more
Only self, self, nothing but self
Greedy, greedier, greediest
Greed, greediness
Men of utmost greed.

MENTAL SLAVERY

Gone, slavery though
But the imprints linger
They torment, they haunt
Hunting even the unborn
Trying to destabilize fate.

Mental slavery, as bad as slavery
Chained mentality
Contaminated thoughts
Mixed feelings; complexity.

Slavery of thoughts
Slavery of movement
Slavery of worship
Slavery of culture
Slavery of tradition
Slavery of models
Slavery of society
Slavery of rules and regulations
Impure choices, indoctrinated.

CRIME

High rate of crime
Games of different lanes
Young and old
Male and female
Children, youths, women.

Crime, gearing up
Towering to the heavens
Normalizing, as norms
Scavengers, abusing life.

Criminals grooming lots
Crimes scaling harlots
Infiltrating the people
Spies on the sky
Crowd in the cloud
Jogging, joggling the jungle.

Courses unknown yet seen
Sources unseen yet known
Voices unheard yet fears
Crimes, cremating
Criminals incriminating.

HUNGER

Hunger in the land
Starvation all over,
Thirst of good things
Wishes dying daily.

Hunger striking children
Lack killing the unborn
Hunger written on faces.

Faces dull, down and dead
Pale, stained and bloody
Hopeless eyes and lips
Needs printed on foreheads.

Hunger, hacking lives
Users, using hunger
Hunger hanging men
Abusers abusing humans.

Hunger hindering humanity
Hovering over lands and climes
Yet, blessed amidst wants.

RICHES

Abundant, riches
Wealth of natural resources
Blessedness of nature
Yet, poor and wretched.

Harnessed and hijacked
Raped and kidnapped
Stripped and whipped
Strangled and suffocated
Choked and smoked,
Bound and tied.

Riches of unequal benevolence
On a platter of gold,
Diamonds and blessings
They double-crossed.

Starved and starving
Starving and salivating
Suffering and smiling
Racial prejudice
Prejudice of men
Men of ungodly mission.

THEY

They are greedy
And dubious,
Self-centered and wicked
They only go for gold
They search for diamond,
They explore oil
And they conquer the people.

Their motive is just wealth
They offer gifts, ungodly gifts
Wrapped with it is slavery,
They bury bondage in it
And coat it with hardship,
They deceive the people
And put them to captivity.

Their intent is conquest
They abduct and capture
They present presents
Presents of deadly contents.

They plant explosives
Physical, mental, spiritual and all kinds,
They are beyond imaginations.

STRATEGY

They use strategies
Strategies that look normal
But actually traps,
These traps catch lands
Lands and nations
Nations and people.

They rule, govern and lead
They manipulate and scatter
They squander and disorganize
They destabilize and sterilize
They are so unkind.

Donations, aids and helps
After strikes, strikings
Tests, tastes and thirsts
Yearnings and yawning
Deceits, deceptions.

Strategies, methods, patterns
Tactics, tricks, pranks
Processes, procedures, protocols
They lay them out from onset
Display of powers.

COMMOTION

They plant commotion
Calculated attempts, written scripts
Actors, manifesting manifestations.

Deaths, hunger and starvations
Violence, turmoil, abuse
Troubles, traumas, dramas
Bundles of ego rubbing
Massages of powers that be.

Commotions of rank and file
Smokes, chokes, pokes
Spit, sputum of lords
Madness, madding crowd
A besieged land.

Trapped in caves
Condemned, betrayed
Frustrated, set-up
Bruised and broken
Battered and murdered
Commotion from powers that be
Houses on the rock going down.

RELIGION

Different religions
Professing love and hate
But living hate.

Numerous faiths
Raising faithfuls and followers
Yet, ill-fated.

Too many sermons
Incredible teachings
Actually brainwashing
Indoctrination of horrors.

Religious leaders and bigots
Sweeping across the world
Rolling away unity
Blowing off oneness.

Religious and religionists
Binding regions and legions,
Yet, singing godliness.

MISPLACED AGGRESSION

Foreign powers remoting
Local people lifting
Strange voices speaking
Rural persons hearing
Aliens, ordering
Aborigines, fighting.

Misplaced aggression
Rage from induced hate
Used and uselessness
Remoting, pressing, timed
Buttons and surveillance
Arrangements and settlements,
People akin to using others.

Olden foundations
Colonized principles
Laws of unafrican rules
Imposed, superimposed.

Transferred aggression
Anger and angst
Heavy yoke on a weak neck.

EXPERIMENTS

Engaging people in trials
Using them for tests
Carrying out inhuman missions
Causing mayhem
Causing havoc.

Boiling lies and stories
Digging for troubles
Extracting sorrows
Exhuming wickedness
Exhibiting pretense.

Falling down on them
Crushing them to pieces
Yet, mourning louder and harder
Appearing useful and needful
While being the demon.

Experiments of billions
Infiltrating, covering up
Unspeakable and despicable acts
Turning people against themselves
Shattering their tables
And watching them burn.

CRIME

Crime becoming deals
Growing wings
Flying with credits,
And shunting peace.

Crime, stealing joy
Duping love and care
Strangling oneness
Torturing unity
Blocking goals.

Crime, enveloping
Eloping with freedom
Spoiling toils
Boiling oils
Quashing authenticity.

Crime, leaking secrets
Rolling up nationhood
Scattering foundations
And laying nets
Nets for horrendous evil.

SEX

Now, a talent
A drive like no other
Serious inventions
Insane discoveries,
Excess announcements
Loud adverts
Bold sales and markets
Sex, like no other.

Open sex, public sex
Secret sex, forbidden sex
Rape, forceful, horrible
Transmissions of diseases
Intentional spread of ill.

No age limit
No barrier
At will, however
Looks like tournaments
Bundles of recklessness
Activities so cruel and worldly
Unkind fellows devouring
Unsafe land emerging.

HIV AIDS

Diseases on display
So rampant, surging
HIV in vogue
Aids trending
Forcing people for sex.

Hundreds of victims
Unsafe parents,
Sick children
Dead land.

HIV Aids on the rise
From mother to child
From husband to wife,
From boyfriend to girlfriend
From friend to friend.

HIV Aids spreading
Perching on heads unknown
Settling on lives known
Ripping the land of health
Lifelessness crowning future.

RAPE

Victims hide not
Victims sex more
Intentional contacts
Giving it at will.

Rape, raping lives
Severing eyes and hope
Sealing future.

Rape at peak
Horrible urge and ransack
Raiding hoods and cities
Sharing fliers of ill.

Rape, victims, victims of rape
Helpless and hopeless
Cursed, accursed
Duped, defeated.

Rape, crime, evil
The king of lives
The ruler of men
The devourer of the land.

LAZINESS

Lazy and ignorant
Backward and wayward
Ungodly and uncultured.

Waiting for manner
Stealing from oxen
Overloading carmels
Burdening donkeys.

Greedy and selfish
Closed minds and poor
Unkind and un-cheerful
Impolite, impatient, ingrate.

Lazy to the bone
Fighting hard workers
Killing workaholics
Stoning strangers
Coining it freedom.

ASSASSINATION

Hate has no boundary
It breeds anger and rage
Bitterness to do evil.

Assassination and killings
Stars and superstars
Murdering of heroes
Intentionally and unintentionally.

It seems joyful
It seems planned
It appears lawful
It appears supported,
Assassination of mouth pieces.

Not one, not two
Men of valour
Men of strength
Exemplary men,
Patriotic men
National voices
Local and rural
Known and unknown.

GANGSTERISM

Gangs of young men
Living in crime
Dwelling in criminality
Menace to the society.

Gangsters and gangsterism
Rivals and rivalries
Contests and contestants
Protests and Protestants
Competition, complexity
Inferiority and superiority
Choking the land
Suffocating the people
Toxic and toxicity
Intoxicating humans.

Gangsterism and godfatherism
Godfathers backing atrocity
Patrons supporting
Direct and indirect backups,
Values, degrading
Norms, depreciating
Cultures, eroding.

MARRIAGE

Marriage procreates
It sustains mankind
And prolongs humanity.

Strangers fall in love
They marry your own
They reproduce, recreate and procreate
Hoping to maintain lineages.

But somewhere, somehow
They lose, they lose
They lose properties and monies
They lose lives, lives, lives
They even lose their lives.

If marriage was forbidden
If you like not strangers
If you want no international
Why yielding in to marriage.

Killing in-laws, leaving children fatherless
Your own grandchildren
Your own children,
Your blood.

MINERS

They kill miners
They frustrate them
They pay them poorly
They deny them their rights.

Miners weep, cry and mourn
Miners shout, wail and pray
But barely are they heard.

Miners in deep agony
Calling on powers for salvation
Pleading with authorities for rescue
Wishing better for themselves.

Strange foreigners own them
They own rights and license,
Local foreigners work hard
Dying inside mines.

Miners, young and old
Voiceless strugglers
Gaining little or nothing
As manipulations live on their labour.

RACISM

Black and blackness
Poor and poorness
Low and lowness
Hate and hatefulness
Bitter and bitterness
Unhappy and unhappiness
Exchange of a breed.

Racism, black on black
Racism, black on white
Racism, white on black
Prejudice and injustice
Slight on nature.

Power tussle, giants
Two elephants fighting
Suffering the grasses
Killing grasshoppers
Crushing butterflies
Beautiful and colourful
Natural and blessed ants
Bearing brunt of wars.

PROMISCUITY

Waywardness and lawlessness
Lust and indiscriminate sex
Lack of self esteem
Blindness and darkness.

Sexual activities
Sex slaves and sex objects,
Human trafficking.

Promiscuity, carelessness
Abortion and illegitimate children
Single mothers surging
Baby mama and sugar daddies.

Recklessness and waywardness
Huge energy in immorality
Extravagant activities
Clubbing and drugging
Cycles and circles
Illwinds, whirlwinds
Hurricanes of harmful future.

SINGLE PARENTING

Abandoned children
Fatherless, single mothers
Battles within and without
Lack, want, need, poverty.

Out of school
Poor nutrition
Porous rearing
Empty training,
Dark orientation
Traumatic upbringing
Chances of societal ill.

Single parenting
Loose love, firmless care
Purging statutes, killing
Bruised and broken
Lost identity, fear of the unknown.

Heavy duties, weak hand
Strong forces, feeble stands
Single parenting, abounding
Results of some ridiculous actions.

PROSTITUTION

Men and women, young and old
Sacrificing their bodies,
Internal and external
Terminating many things
Contracting so much.

Prostituting for fun and money
Trying to make ends meet
Chasing fame, cheering harm.

As though legal
As if normal
As of radical
Nuances and nuisances.

Chains and cartels
Cliques and cabals
Up and above
Down and below
Known and unknown
Seen and unseen,
Heard and unheard
Traders, trading on humanity.

MIGRATION

Migration is not a crime
People move from place to place
In search of greener pasture.

My people say a proverb
No one stays at a place
To watch masquerade-occasion,
Migration is part of life
No one stays at a spot forever.

People move, humans travel
For various reasons
Education, tourism, employment
Entertainment, marriage, transfers, and others.

No laws say people should not travel
We embrace change daily,
We learn, we grow, we adapt, we adopt
We adjust, we readjust too.

Besides, no people can totally survive alone
Relationship is diverse,
We need each other in life.

EDUCATION

Education is necessary
It builds the society
It enlightens the world
And disperses darkness.

Education unravels timidity
And broadens visions,
It helps survival
And prolongs quest.

Education manages resources
Both natural and artificial,
It creates wealth
It sustains growth
It supports development
And maintains integration.

However, miseducation is evil
It kills, it butchers, it condemns
Illiteracy is a scum
It taunts and haunts,
Uneducated people can be deadly
Ignorant folks can cause mayhem.

IGNORANCE

Ignorance is a disease
It is highly contagious,
It decimates and debases.

Ignorance is an epidemic
It spreads, it chokes
It is a big burden.

Ignorance is a yoke
It is heavy, it is dangerous
It blinds and blindfolds.

Ignorance is a chain
It depicts slavery,
Dark age and dark ages
It portrays backwardness.

Ignorance is deadly
It has brainwashed many,
And it is brainwashing many
Misinterpretation, misunderstanding
Wiping out races
Sealing off generations.

IMMORALITY

The society is decayed
Moral decadence, rising
Sinful acts growing
Lustful actions multiplying
Abominations, being welcomed
Taboos, normalizing
Sacrileges, initializing
Desecration of highest orders
All and more frolicking together.

Immoralities, inhumane activities
Disrespect, disregard, dishonesty, distrust
Betrayal, lies, slanders
Scandals, rumours, propagandas
Deceitful and vengeful acts
All, towering to the sky.

Nothing is sacred anymore
Consecrated things are destroyed
Holy things are vain,
The land is so desolate
Affliction of iniquity
Affliction and iniquity
Immorality, a living god.

MENACE

The society is stinking and sinking
Menace is in the palace
Touts and pickpockets
Vagabonds and cultists
Criminals and dupers
Killers, assassins, murderers
Prostitutes, drug pushers and addicts
Wasting lives and lands.

Menace in every place
Messing with grace
Denting innocent face
At a high pace
Fighting to win the race.

A conscious speed
Full of greed
Unwanted weed
Corrupting every breed.

Menace, menace, menace
In a very despicable manner
Roaring like lion.

ENVY

Sometimes, envy creeps in
It destabilizes good heart
It shakes happy soul
And deceives poor spirit.

Envy contributes
Yes, it does
It harms friendship
And ruins relationship.

When a visitor excels
When he succeeds
When he labours more
And his efforts pay off
Envy gathers to kill.

Envy harbours evil
It circulates evil throughout,
And burns red candles
It dims lights
And shares darkness,
Envy, many a time rages
Yes, it stops strangers.

GREENER PASTURE

When home is dry and empty
When home is dark and slippery
When home is neither free nor fair
When home is poor and wretched,
One tends to look for greener pasture.

Greener pasture can be anywhere
As long as it is not where forbidden,
When home is lonely and boring
When home is cruel and harsh
When home is old and rugged,
When home is crude and haggard
When home is lean and lanky
One would be tempted for greener pasture.

When home is dirty and untidy
When home is unkempt and unclean
When it is harmful and hot
When it is hungry and angry
When it is thirsty and nasty
One could be forced to look elsewhere.

Greener pasture anywhere
Anyhow, anytime, with anything
Because humans need life and love.

SACRIFICE

Many sacrifice a lot
Yes, families do
They sell certain things and belongings
They borrow, they buy
They work, they labour
They forfeit, they denounce
They do a lot, a whole lot
To send people overseas.

They place their hope on them
They pray and long and wait
They ponder and wonder
They nurture dreams
And they believe it will happen.
When home is good and great
When home is real and ready,
When home is prepared and organized
No one migrates unnecessarily.

Families sacrifice a lot
They do crazy things to live
They believe these sacrifices are their survival.

FOREIGN CONTROL

Foreign control is not in the street
Not the employees
Not the labourers,
Not the shop-owners
Not the hawkers
They are invisible
Yet, visible.

Foreign control rules
They lead and manipulate
They decide, they govern
They are cartels and cabals
They own blocks and mines
They own gold, diamonds
They control economies
Invisible and invincible.

Foreigners are many
Some lead, some follow
Some cook, some eat
Some labour, some suffer
Some dictate, some decide
Not all foreigners are threats.

OBSERVERS

As they cause trouble
They sit back and watch
They wine and dine
And cheer and merry.

They scramble over gold
Other people's gold,
They grab diamonds
Other people's diamonds,
They set up war
And locals fight it up.

Observers far away
Holding the toning fork,
Toning fork of trouble.

Observers near, around
Within the bloodshed
Shooting at everyone
Randomly at will.

They are snipers
They are hidden,
Yet conspicuous
They are not far
But some come from afar.

COVETOUSNESS

They are rich, very rich
They are exposed too
They travel far and wide,
They touch the sky
They live in heavens
They hold the clouds
They occupy the planets
They announce discoveries
They make the news
They cause stories
Yet, they are ambitious.

Not contented, not satisfied, never
Wicked adventures, ungodly creations
Greedy purchases
Covetousness, gathering all.

Covetousness, taking by force
Violation, exploitation, humiliation
Time bombs, traps, and cages
Willingly enslaving people
Scavengers with gifts
Gifts to take even more.

CAVEMEN

Cavemen in caves
Lions in the jungles
Surviving at all cost
Carnivorous talibans.

Archaic, old and outdated
Obsolete, ancient and timid
Primitive, crude and raw
Hating freedom and emancipation
Warding off change.

Cavemen, poor and poor
Marking time, backward
Never moving forward
Aligning not with hope.

Bunch of sociopaths
Needing rehabilitation
Avoiding progress
Pushing down faith
Cavemen, a breed of monsters.

REHABILITATION

Some are brainwashed
Some are drugged
Some are drunk
Some are initiated
Some are bonded
Some are bound
Some are indoctrinated,
Many, many, need rehabilitation.

Physical torture
Mental torture
Financial slavery
Political slavery,
Academic bondage
Moral bondage
Social punishment,
They need rehabilitation.

Lifelessness, uselessness
Poverty, lack and need
Scarcity of help
There is need for rehabilitation.

POVERTY

Poverty thriving
People striving
Hunger surviving
Sex driving
Death diving.

Poverty, poverty, poverty
Poorness and poorness
Poorly poor, poorest of the poor
Poverty, a trigger to hate.

A road to stealing
A strike to wanting
A track to lying
A push to robbing
A path to lust
Poverty, it bears many children.

Alleviate poverty
Elevate the people
Kill poverty
Emancipate the land.

GOVERNMENT

The government is many
They define, describe and decide
They pick according to choice
They make sure it suits them.

The government is real
They make deal
They serve meal
And make people heal
But then they conceal.

Stories, stories, news
People lose interest in them
They dissociate their trust
They remove their faith
Because government is funny.

They fail, they connive
They manipulate, they manoeuvre
So the people take laws into their hands.

If governments maintain
If they govern purely,
If they rule orderly
The world would be safe.

FALSE PROMISES

False promises up and down
From different tiers of government
False implementations and actions
From different arms of government
All, add to worries and horrors.

Being severally lied to
Being deceived always
Being fooled all the time
Being mistreated now and then
All, boost crime and criminality.

Nothing works, nothing supports
Lies and lies, false promises
Hateful speeches, deceptive voices
Playful manifestations, dubious acts
Events and occasions of selfishness
All, brew evil in the land.

False hope, false answers
False promises, false actions
False faith, false future
The government appears false.

CARELESSNESS

To your tents O citizens
Go and cater for yourselves
Look away from authorities
Stay put in your pain.

To your tents O citizens
Fight your fight
Bear your cross
The yoke is yours
Heavy or light
Suit yourselves.

To your tents O citizens
Never complain, live or die
Never hesitate, keep struggling
Feed your anger, feed it
Starve your soul, starve it
Kill your spirit, kill it
Murder your heart, murder it
Burn your love, burn it
Bury your unborn, bury it
Just stay far away from us.

We are careless
We are mean,
We care not
We fear not,
To hell with you all.

LOOSENESS

Looseness, here and there
Waywardness on the rise
Blind eye to crime,
Facing enjoyment abroad.

Looseness, creating gaps
Gaps harbouring evil
Openings, wrong openings
Loopholes, thick and thin
Sinking the mighty ship.

Forget it, face front
Mind your business
Political correctness
Talk, say it, reveal it
Do or die, die or do, do and die
Loose, looseness, loosen.

Loosened, loosing, loosening
Looseness in a land of gold
Gold burning, melting lives
Severing brothers and bonds
Manipulators, family crime.

MANDELA

Mandela, Madiba
Father of leadership
Born to lead.

Madiba, Mandela
Man of the people
The people's president.

Mandela, the human-god
The hero-legend-giant
The name, the anchor.

The redeemer, the fighter
The emancipator, the leader
The black, the blackness.

He cried, he suffered
He wept, he fought
He rallied, he gathered
He beckoned, he pleaded
He was heard, he was freed
Freed, freed indeed.

APARTHEID

Apartheid was horrible
It multiplied sorrow
It cooked torment
And served torture.

Apartheid was terrible
It boiled hate
And planted slavery,
It garnished bigotry
And banished freedom.

Apartheid, it was cruel
It hanged, it killed
It mutilated, it butchered
It buried, it burned
It bombed, it raped
It was demonic.

Apartheid was satanic
It ruled freeborn
And enslaved kings
It bound princes
And captured queens,
Apartheid, finally defeated.

CONTRIBUTIONS

Nigeria wept, she cried
Nigeria prayed and fasted
Nigeria hungered and thirsted
Nigeria fought and won.

Nigeria contributed
Young and old
Men and women,
Children, pupils and students
Workers, everyone.

Nigeria, bore it all
Artists, prophets, actors
Philosophers, prayer warriors,
Aids, thinkers, singers, brotherhood.

Nigeria fought apartheid
Nigeria won apartheid,
Loud, bold, strong and proud.

YOUNG

No matter the greenness
No matter the milk
No mater the honey
Irrespective of the fertility
No matter the natural resources
You are still young.

You shine like the sun
And glow like the moon
You twinkle like the star
And flow like the river
But know this, you are young.

Young, a long way to go
Freedom can be lost
Freedom can be bondage,
It can be caged
So beware you are young.

Youthful exuberance can kill
Pride goes before a fall
And the fall falls deep truly.

LEGITIMATE

Many are legitimate
Many are legal
Many are law abiding
Many are peaceful,
Why torment them?

The ones who are real
Who look for no trouble
Who do normal work
Who obey and respect,
Why kill them?

Why harm all
Why victimize everyone
Why chase them away
Why vowing to do horror?

Your are outside too
Yours are everywhere as well
They do good, bad
They live hard, soft
Who knows tomorrow?

JEALOUSY

Strangers do not stop you
Strangers do not bind you
They hijack not your business
They chase you not away
Do not get jealous.

Jealousy is bad
It does more harm than good
Get up and keep going
Do not hide under laziness.

Strangers can help, they heal
Strangers can build, they lit
Strangers can save, they give
Join with them, love them
For we are all strangers somewhere.

Jealousy is a cancer
It breeds death
Jealousy is a cankerworm
It rips off sanity.

ROBBERY

Anybody can rob
Robbers come from anywhere
It depends on individuals.

Robbery is a crime
And should be treated as such
By legal authorities,
Why taking laws into your hands?

Many 'thieves' are innocent
Many of them are pure
Just that we hated them
Just that we targeted them
Just that we set them up
Just that we never listened,
They became victims of hate.

Robbers are humans
They deserve humanity
Not animalistic treatment,
Some can become better
No matter who they are.

DRUG ABUSE

Drug abuse is a menace
It destroys the society
It scatters the future
The future of the society,
And leaves addicts shattered.

Drug abuse is dangerous
It kills, it wastes
It shocks, it dwindles
Lives built on drugs derail
They are harmful and shady.

But if we hate drugs
If we hate the abuse
If we need it not
If we want it stopped and eradicated
It we want a clean environment
If our society is dear to us,
If we are sincere and honest
If we are truthful to ourselves
If we owe our unborn sanity
If we want a better world
We can curb all these harmful issues.

But we are selfish
We are insincere and insensitive
We are greedy and materialistic
Ungodly and disloyal, hence we continue suffering.

USERS AND ABUSERS

Users and abusers
Users are many
Abusers are numerous,
Users are locals
Abusers are locals,
Users are strangers
Abusers are strangers,
Users and abusers
A web so complex and complicated.

Drug users and abusers
Robbers and gangsters
Rapists and criminals
Thieves and killers,
They are users and abusers
They are locals and strangers
Intertwined, interwoven.

Evil is not tribal
Good is not racial
Humanity is not religious
Unity is not cultural
They all are sandwiched.

Secret users, unknown abusers
Business tycoons,
Players and game changers
Scrabblers scrambling, scribbling
Unseen and unreadable notes,
Behind the scene.

OWNERS

People own farms
People own mines
People own wells
People own groups
These people influence all.

They own drug laws
They tip off and tip in
They make real currencies.

People own mines
They license, they revoke
They control, they despatch
They create wealth.

People own wells
They explore, they extract
They produce money.

People own groups
Different types of group
They front whoever
They hide wherever
They do whatever.

DIPLOMACY

Diplomacy, an elder
A reckless adult
Pretending to be calm
Trying to be logical
But truly Cumming.

Wearing a mask
Hardening the task,
Creating some scene
Appearing obscene.

Diplomacy, a trap tricky
An adult prank
Perching on branches like birds
Singing lullabies to babies
Cooling the fight,
Igniting the war.

Blind eye, wickedness
Pretense, hide and seek
Partner in crime
Accomplice, diplomatic
Diplomatic accomplice.

SUDDENLY

Yes, suddenly
Suddenly, something will happen
Minor thing so weightless
It will escalate into arguments
From there challenges,
Then fights and troubles.

Yea, suddenly
You will hear voices
Shouts and shootings
Guns and gunshots
Cries and crying
Murders and murdering
Yes, suddenly
In a twinkle
A mob gathers.

Destructions, stabbings
Killings, running, chasing
Civilians, officials, men, women
In a twinkle, nations versus nations
Deaths, deaths and fears.

ATTACKS

They would mobilize
With weapons and clubs
Moving from place to place
Searching for escapees
Beating them up and killing them.

Freedom, free at will
Free for all
Doing whatever pleases them
No powers to stop or subdue them.

Cheering and fanning
With progressively higher voices
From powers that be.

They attack at will
Randomly, yet targeted
Mobs, mobbing foreigners.

Destroying lives and properties
Ordering killings and lootings
Taking spoils and spoiling
With authorities either afar off
Or indirectly supporting.

Silent, dumb, cheerful
Loud, conspicuous, joyous
Hurting generations born and unborn.

BURNING

They burn down shops
They set businesses ablaze
They raze down properties,
Properties of foreigners.

They crush everything
Anything within reach
They turn them into ashes.

Young men, able-bodied
Destroying sweat and strength
Unleashing anger on dwellings
Dwellings of zeal and passion.

Deriving joy in harming
Rejoicing for doing evil
Crossing limits and boundaries,
Chasing away rivers of blessing.

Yes, they burn enterprises and entrepreneurs
They burn homes and houses
They burn lives.

LOOTING

They loot in and out
They loot food and materials
They loot people's sweat.

Sweat built over ages
Properties under sleepless nights
Acquisition of great sufferings,
They share them
They loot happily
They cart them away
No one stops them.

Looting, by men and women
Hungry, greedy, jealous
Envious, covetous, lazy
They loot tomorrow.

As if freedom
As if law
As if government
As if supported,
They loot, they burn
They kill, they destroy.

WOMEN

Girls, ladies and women
Females of different ages
They loot, they kill
They murder, they burn.

They burn humans
Women that born,
Women that love
Women that care
Women that save
Women that protect,
Women that culture
Women that nurture,
Yes, they join in burning humans alive.

They stone, they loot
They burn, they mock
They butcher, they destroy
Women, the gods on earth.

Dancing, enjoying, laughing
Yelling, cheering, cursing
Stoning, fanning, unbelievable women.

SETTING HUMANS ABLAZE

They set people ablaze
They burn them to ashes
They rejoice and merry
As fellow humans burn.

What manner of people burn humans
What makes a land so cruel
Why are they so crude
Why do they enjoy killing,
People toasting over dying people
People partying over burning humans,
What makes them so inhumane?

People burn, people smile
People bleed, people laugh
People cry, people clap
Dancing on skulls
Jumping on graves,
Like a festival
As cameras roll.

BUTCHERING STRANGERS

They butcher brothers
They cut flesh
They spill blood,
They salute.

Blood of friends
Blood of colleagues
Blood of visitors
Blood of black men.

Skulls in pieces
Hearts, ripped off
Leg, hands, dismembered
They love death
So they make corpses.

They kill anyhow
They have no rules
They are carnivorous
They prefer blood.

Their government watches
Their leaders cool off
Their rulers fuel it,
Their utterances mean so
They kill with speed.

STONING

Stoning, stoning humans
Not martyrs this time
But strangers.

Sinful, holy or not
Caught, red-handed
Suspected or not,
Guilty or innocent
Proven or unclear
True or false,
Stoning makes them happy.

Bricks, concretes
Large stones of heavy weight
Crushing victims
Hitting their heads
Never merciful,
Bent on killing
Killing their fellow blacks.

Concretes, bricks, heavy
Mighty, big and scary
Stoning them like Stephen
Enjoying the play
Shooting though like a movie
They merry at killing foreigners
Especially Nigerians,
The Nigeria that saved them from apartheid.

LAWLESS

Powers say they are powerless
Laws say they are lawless
Leaders say they lead no one
Followers say they follow their will
Everyone to their fate.

The land rejects strangers
A certain type, from a certain place
The rivers swallow them
The air abhors visitors
The gates dispel them,
But these strangers help them when in need.

Lawless, mannerless, cultureless
Loveless, lifeless, fearless, fearful
Ungodly, unfair, inhumane
They take laws into their hands,
Their hands, full of blood.

Powers applaud, laws align
Leaders alure, followers act
Strangers die, visitors burn
The land is doomed.

Fears amidst mourning
Africa moans in deep labour,
No one knows what she will birth.

INJUSTICE

Injustice, inhumanity
Erring citizens get cautioned
Laws are there
Suspects get arrested and tried
Criminals are arraigned
Guilty people get punished
According to the law,
Be they natives or strangers.

But not here
They are the system
They are the law
They serve justice
Based on hate, prejudice and ignorance.

Injustice everywhere
North, south, east, west
Up, down, front, back.

No one cares to know
Not minding it is a small world
Karma and nemesis
Consequences and repercussions,
Because what goes around comes around.

Injustice hatching, incubating
Breeding a monster and a ghost
A ghost that would ruin the land forever.

POLICE

Police aiding crime
Sometimes starting it
Laughing at corpses
Questioning burning men
Interrogating dead bodies,
Mocking men turning into ashes.

Smiling police officers
Smiling at people set ablaze,
Looting police officers
Looting with looters.

Forces that protect
Becoming forces that kill,
Forces that defend
Becoming forces that destroy.

Men and women watching people burn
Watching them cry, wail, weep, scream,
Watching them die a painful death
Happy, joyful, fulfilled
Police watch and aid horror.

Hopes burning, dreams dying
Futures screaming, generations going down
Humans dance and merry.

CORPSES

Corpses return home
Lucky ones, lucky families
Cargoes flying them home.

Virtually weekly, monthly
Corpses return, pride of families
Sent, travelled for greener pasture.

Hale and hearty men
Future leaders and heroes
Young men that left in peace
Returning in pieces,
Scars, marks, mutilated bodies.

Corpses for courses
Corpses without causes
Corpses beyond curses.

They fly home, they end
Many young and unmarried
Many childless, fruitless
Dead, gone and forgotten.

Migration, search for greener pasture
For better life and health
For education, exposure and wealth;
Corpses return in their place.

UNWELCOME

When people are no more loyal
When strangers misbehave
When they overstay their welcome
When they defile your gods
When they desecrate your shrines
When they constitute nuisance
When they become threats
Glaring threats, understandable
Reasonable harms,
Legally deal with them.

Lands have laws
Nations have rules
Humans have boundaries
Humanity has limits,
There are bearable things
There are unbearable ones,
When foreigners err
The laws should prevail.

The legal system is there
The judiciary is there,
Why stone, butcher, kill strangers?

BAD GOVERNANCE

If government was good
If all was well,
If leaders truly led
If rulers actually ruled
If agencies were real
People would be stable,
And the world at large.

Deliberately suffering the people
Intentionally manipulating the land
Brutally dismantling
Boundlessly disengaging the people,
Ungodly hardening life.

Bad governance all over
From top to down, down to top
Left, right, center
All nooks and crannies.

A reflection of the people
A reflection of the government,
Bad governance, bad people
Good governance, good people.

SHAMELESS LIES

They tell lies, bold lies
They cook lies, white lies
They despatch lies, horrors
Lies, glittering lies
Insane lies, so inhuman.

Men of timber and calibre
Role models, custodians
Rulers and leaders
Agents of light, hope
They lie woefully.

Bitter lies, uncalled for
The land knows the truth
The world sees the truth,
Unnecessary lies, they fabricate
The unborn speaks it
The dead is a witness
Yet, they lie, they twist
They tell fairy tales,
Tales of laughable stories.

Shameless people, lying desperately
Telling desperate lies to dying people,
Mocking the dead with wickedness.

HOSTAGE

Some children at home
Away from school for safety
Their parents hiding
Away from business for safety
Because they are being hunted.

Held hostage to self
For death to pass
Actually held hostage by mob,
Against self, they hide
Because they are the target.

Angry mobs descending
Chanting in one voice
Go home, go home, go home.

A land rescued from others
A people spared by brotherhood
A young, delivered from slavery.

See them inviting bondage
See them killing love
Look, they bury unity
Because when all go home
They would turn their arrows against themselves.

BLACK ON BLACK HATE

The killing is specific
They go for blacks
They beat them up
They stone them to death.

They butcher some
They stab, they burn
And gyrate around the bonfire.

Black on black hate
Crisis, killings, burnings
Only on, against blacks
From blacks that saved them.

A land fought for
A people spoken for,
A country saved
A tribe guarded and guided,
A race stood with.

Blacks killing fellow blacks
Stoning them in an era like this
Burning them to ashes
Destroying their sweat and businesses
In a broad daylight,
In a world fast developing.

ORGANIZED CRIME

It sounds crazy
That bodies cool off
Authorities watch on
And lives waste down.

It looks organized
It sounds supported,
It seems arranged
It tells collusive
It means acceptance,
A land so dearly fought for.

General help from Africa
With Nigeria on the lead
Monies, resources, sacrifices
Manpower, prayers, songs
Delegations, demonstrations, petitions
Rejections, withdrawals, submissions
Losses, passion, seriousness, dedication
Commitments, pronouncements
Loyalty, love, oneness, support
A people so liberated.

Drug, prostitution, human trafficking
Organ harvesting, hate, racism,
Crimes, no matter what be they
Can be arrested if not aided.

AGONY

Agony abounds, yes
They are numerous
Some are avoidable
Some are controllable
Some are natural
Some are manmade,
The worst is the latter.

Watching your business burn down
Looking at touts set you ablaze
Begging mobs to spare your life
Beckoning on looters to help you
With all falling on deaf ears,
These agonies are worst.

Helplessly watching them kill yours
Running helter skelter to no avail
Trying to save your own
Shouting for rescue,
Calling on gods and deities for justice
Yet, losing everything
These agonies are wickedness.

Hate, greed, envy, jealousy
Diplomats of an ungrateful world.

SHAME

The people that raped your land
The ones that dehumanized you
The ones that enslaved you
The ones that tortured you
You never burnt them alive.

They took your lands and mines
They sold your gold and cotton
They mined your diamonds
They owned your soil
Yet, they are safe.

You stoop so low
Lower than the ground
To harm, hurt and kill
Your brothers, your own.

Tactics, diplomacy, methods, patterns
They move, they encroach, they take over
With gifts, gifts of deception
With sweet tongues and promises
With games and plays,
They occupy, they advance, they annex.

Shame on you, shame
Shame, if the system is evil
Shame, if the law is dead
Shame, if you live on jungle justice
Shame, if you remain unchangeable
Shame, if slavery still enslaves you
Shame, if blood gives you peace.

REPRISAL ATTACKS

Reprisal attacks are bitter
They could be deadlier,
Once beaten, twice shy
Thrice beaten, forever shy.

When people are pushed to the wall
Over and over and over again,
They react, they act, they repel
They can do or die or do and die.

No one has the monopoly of violence
No one has all the powers on earth,
Anybody could be dangerous
It depends on who chooses to.

Reprisal attacks say much
The messages are ugly
Reprisal attacks tell stories
Stories of swollen anger.

Brothers die, sister mourn
Fathers wail, mothers weep
The lands heat up and melt down
Reprisal attacks, horrors and wars.

KILLINGS

Different methods of killing
Drowning people in hot water
Tying their hands, stoning them
Dragging them along the road
Crushing them on ground,
Hitting them with clubs
Macheting them
Burning them alive.

Wickedness, heartlessness
Strangers, unknown people
Instantly being enemies
Just because of where they come from
Stereotyping, assumptions, beliefs,
Wrong conclusions, closed minds.

Killing of most inhumane nature
As if we were never humans
Being entertained by death
Videoing, taking photos and pictures of assaults
Cheering and enjoying horrors
Clapping for killers
Hailing murderers,
Laughing at voices that plead for mercy.

Gleeful scene, meanness
Beyond barbarism
Satanic and demonic,
A people so ungodly backward.

Some holy books emphasized on treatment of strangers
Some religions teach on welcoming of strangers
Some prophets and thinkers taught on strangers
We follow them, we hear them, we learn them
We all have religions and holy books,
Yet, so cruel and wicked.

XENOPHOBIA

Xenophobia, fear of strangers
Strong fear and phobia
A large antipathy towards strangers
Even harmless strangers.

Phobia for their brilliance
Phobia for their progress
Phobia for their strength
Phobia for their breakthrough
Phobia for their advancement.

Xenophobia, silent and calm
Silent in some worlds
Calm in some climes
Unknown in some areas
Except in South Africa.

Open, loud, crystal clear
Whether a ritual or sacrifice
If not less than quarterly, biannually, annually
Xenophobia, fear of strangers
Mobid hate, hate, hate
Strangers, unknown, known, young, old, unborn.

MEANWHILE

Meanwhile you live everywhere
Your citizens travel around and abroad,
They live undisturbed.

They study, tour and visit
They invest, explore and live
They manipulate and manoeuvre too.

They build empires and empires
They cruise and cruise
They live in luxuries and luxuriously,
They do like others as well.

Meanwhile they fly up and down
They start, they stop
They begin, they advance
They move on, that way.

Uncountable trips abroad
Various businesses untold
Numerous lifestyles of course
They are as normal as others
They hardly get molested
Except the law finds them guilty.

NIGERIA

In Nigeria, alone
Your businesses thrive
Merchandise and franchise.

Our population pays you
Millions of dollars circulate
They circulate in your circle,
You generate billions.

Mobile networks, MTN
DSTV Cable networks
Reality TV Shows
Banks, Shoprite
Uncountable businesses
Permits, licenses, and rights
All flowing through Nigeria.

Some abuse, and violate
Some breach and disappoint
Deceits, lies, partial duping and fraud
Poor services and network failures
Blind eyes sustain those deals.

Milking our land, degrading us
Then killing us when we visit
Where is Africa and Africanness?

BORDERS

If borders be closed
If we part ways
If everyone separates
If we be confined
If we become enemies,
Who gains, who loses?

Borders, big or small
Serve a lot, a whole lot
Closed, we suffocate
Open, we breathe
Locked, we choke
Unlocked, we survive
Relationships are beyond here.

Gold and silver perish
Diamond and oil, finish
Unity and strength survive
Peace and love grow,
Nothing ever outlives mankind.

QUALIFICATIONS

Taking your jobs?
When one is qualified
He is likely to get the job.

When one is unqualified
Chances are he will not get the job.

Strangers taking your jobs, possible?
Professionals do professional things.

Cleaners are not nurses
Drivers are not doctors
Gardeners are not lawyers
People work where they fit in.

Qualifications tell it all
Credentials credit people
To everyone, there is an assignment
According to their abilities.

Upgrade, advance, learn, study
Grow, change, embrace, adapt
Welcome, be humane enough
Humanity is not for monsters.

I AM BECAUSE YOU ARE

Ubuntu, you preach
Ubuntu, you sing
I am because you are
You are because I am.

Where then is Ubuntu
If I am gone
And you are here?

Once we cried for your pain
Now, we cry for the pain you cause us
Over sixty billion spent on apartheid
According to African Standard paper, to save you.

Ubuntu, Ngumuntu
Ngabantu, you must serve your fellow man
Mandiba warned, Mandela reiterated,
But now you kill, you kill them.

We are only people because of others
Take upon yourself where you live
To make others joyful and full of hope,
Remember fools multiply when wise people keep silent,
Mandela always emphasized.

FEW PEOPLE

Except for the few
The few who spoke out
The few condemning it,
God bless them.

They were humans and humane enough
Whether educated or not
They understood the consequences
The evil in killing,
The repercussions and after effects.

They condemned it
Some made videos, some cried
Some prayed, some never supported it
May God bless them.

Wherever they are
Whatever they do
Anything they pray for,
Whenever they need
May God answer them,
May they prosper
For standing out, speaking loud
Against atrocities
Atrocities of their people.

May the living bless them
May the dead favour them,
May the unborn love them
May the earth hearken to their plea always.

DEAD ONES

We pray for them
Victims of xenophobia
South African xenophobia
May they rest in peace.

May they find peace
May their rest be well
May they forgive the living
May they be welcomed in heaven
May they have no reason to die again.

However, they were killed
Whenever and anywhere in South Africa
May they forgive those who failed them;
Home and abroad
May their rest be divine.

If things were smooth
If home was blissful
 If the land was green,
If the future was bright
They might not have travelled
To uplift and upgrade
Only to return in corpse.

We will never forget
We will always remember
We owe you these tributes.

STRANDED

Stranded, helpless and hopeless
Ashamed, worried and confused
We know there are still some.

Stranded, may be hidden
Lost, doubtful and lonely
Bored, disappointed and fearful,
We know they exist.

For those who may never return
Those who have lost interest in life
Those who hate home
Those who run, run, and run
Because of issues, issues, unfathomable
We pray for you still.

May God give you hope
May He rebuild you
May He unite your heart, body and soul
May He ignite your love and passion
May He protect and guide you
May the future bless you exceedingly.

Stranded souls, stranded souls
Stranded bones, stranded flesh
Scattered, littered, or buried
May you forever find peace.

GO HOME! GO HOME!

Go home! Go home!
Stay and die
Go home! Go home!
Going home glaring.

As death pants and parades
Going home was real
Being chased like rats
Being lynched like goats;
Hunters hunting animals.

No option for many
The only option to some
Even some established, decided
They wanted to go home desperately.

Yes, which way forward
But then a Messiah came
A barrister from the east
The east of Nigeria,
An airline chief executive.

He came, he volunteered
He spearheaded, he supervised
And they came home,
Empty, traumatized, dramatized
Like a dream, they forfeited all.

ALLEN ONYEMA

The saviour came
Allen Onyema, the barrister
A business mogul
The peaceful man of air peace.

He stood up for Nigerians
Yes, he claimed and reclaimed his people
It did not matter the names they called them
He vowed to evacuate them all
As many as all that want to return to Nigeria.

Willing to come back?
Put the bill on me
He spent millions of Naira
He sacrificed with his crew
They did their best,
Their utmost best.

He met with bodies
Delays, denials and trials
Lies, harassments and embarrassments,
He evacuated them
They returned and reunited.

Batch by batch, one by one
Women and children, men
Young, old, great and small
They returned, they were airlifted.

The mark, clear, conspicuous
Indelible, unforgettable, unfortunate
Like war fronts and war times
My people were evacuated from South Africa.

AIR PEACE

Air peace, peaceful
With strong campaign
Yet, against xenophobia.

Wonderful head
Excellent crew
Professional airline.

They took the pain
They took the joy
They sacrificed, they served
They saved, they rescued.

Freely, freely, they worked
Timelessly, tirelessly
They returned our people in safety
They brought them home
They saved them from death,
They are home, home is god.

Air peace, peaceful air
May the peace of God be with you
May his tranquil always envelop you
Thank you for the salvage,
May you ever be calm
Even in the most troubled world.

VICTIMS

For all victims, we pray
We are with you
Dead or alive, we understand.

For victims over there
Be peaceful, be lawful
Be godly, be loyal
Be humble, be cheerful
Be friendly, be hopeful.

For victims staying back
Look unto God
He will direct you,
Stay away from troubles,
A word is enough for the wise.

A wise man learns from his errors
A wiser man learns from another man's errors
The wisest man learns to not make errors,
Be the wisest man.

xenophobicracy

For those untouched
For those unaffected
May you never see trouble,
May you remain in peace.

Live right, live well
Remember home always
If they no longer want you
Return, home is safe no matter what.

Our love is raw
Undiluted, unflinching, pure and real
Coming home is a wonderful decision.

RETURNEES

Welcome home our people
Thank God who spared you
Welcome, welcome, welcome again
We are happy to see you
We cannot thank God enough.

Life is worth more than rubies
Silver and gold cannot replace you
We are happy you returned.

True, we are in pain
Yes, troubles abound
But home is home, undisputable.

The reality is real, very real
The absurdity is heartbreaking
But we are happy you returned.

Hungry, thirsty, lonely, bored
In lack, in need, in want, in fear
In pain, in life, in death, we are one
We are together, we are with you.

xenophobicracy

Move on, move on, march on
Reintegrate, reunite, reset, restart
The land of your fathers will reestablish you,
Start all over, never be discouraged
Life is all about atempts
Try again, again and again.

You can make it, yes
We will support you
Shoot, hit the target
You are a warrior, a hero
You are indestructible
You survived, you will always do.

AFRICA

Poor Africa, mighty giant
Your gold turns misery
Your diamond is bloody
Your oil is drowning
Your children are dying.

Wars, fights, hate, troubles
East, west, north and south
They manipulate you
They trouble you
Within and without,
They sing for you to fling you.

Usury, anger, bitterness
Sadness, tears, rage,
Look yonder, look yonder
Ponder anew, ponder afresh
Think, pray, work, stand
The world is unfair.

Dear Africa, stand up
Look within, discover
Find out, tear the mask
Who troubles you, who torments you
O Mama Africa
A blessing fearing the world.

Intimidating gifts, divine ladder
Celestial cake, pure encounter
They overturn it, they quash it
Africa dear, push! Push! Push up!

XENOPHOBICRACY

Xenophobia, a fear of strangers
The fear of foreigners.

Xenophobicracy, a fear of the people by the people
against the people.

Xenophobicracy, the fear of strangers by strangers
for strangers, against strangers.

Xenophobicracy, the craziness of people
fearing other people
Destroying other people against other people
for other people.

Xenophobicracy, the fear, the tear, the wear
The gear, the bear, the ear against strangers.

Xenophobicracy, the fear of fearing people
that near you,
And tearing them down, into pieces.

Xenophobicracy, the fear of fearing strangers.

Xenophobicracy, a government that supports xenophobia,
The government of the people that practises xenophobia.

Ngozi Olivia Osuoha is a Nigerian poet, writer and thinker. A graduate of Estate Management with experience in Banking and Broadcasting.

She has sixteen poetry books published in Kenya, Canada, the Philippines, USA, and others. She has also co-authored one (with Kenyan literary critic Amos O. Ojwang').

She has been featured in over sixty-five international anthologies and also has published over two hundred and fifty poems and articles in over twenty countries.

Many of her poems have been translated and published into other languages, including Spanish, Russian, Romanian, Polish, Khloe, Farsi, and Arabic, among others.

She has won many awards; she is a one time *Best of the Net* nominee, and she has numerous words on marble.

colophon

Xenophobicracy, by Ngozi Olivia Osuoha,
was set with Trebuchet MS fonts
by SpiNDec, Port Saint Lucie, Florida
The jacket and covers were designed by
Kris Haggblom, Port Saint Lucie, Florida

www.ingramcontent.com/pod-product-compliance
Lightning Source LLC
Chambersburg PA
CBHW030057100526
44591CB00008B/185